The Fox Twins

Written by Jeanne Willis
Illustrated by Maddy McClellan

It is the fox twins.

I am Jan.
I am Stan.

The fox twins had jam.

I had a lot.
I had **six** pots.

I am sick of jam.
And me.

The twins went to the vet.

The vet must be in.
VET

It is just wind.
Go to bed. And no jam.

Pop!
Putt!
Pop!

Jan fox!
I am not Jan.
I am Stan.
Wink,
wink.

Stan fox!
I am not Stan.
I am Jan.
Wink, wink.

It is a mix up!